The Games

* * *

Harry Josephine Giles

Published by Out-Spoken Press,
Future Studio,
237 Hackney Road,
London, E2 8NA

The right of Harry Josephine Giles to be identified as
the author of this work has been asserted by them in
accordance to section 77of the Copyright, Design and
Patent Act 1988.

A CIP record for this title is available from
the British Library.

First edition published 2018
ISBN: 9781999679200

Design & Art Direction
Ben Lee

Printed & Bound by:
Print Resource

Typeset in: Baskerville

Out-Spoken Press is supported using public
funding by the National Lottery through
Arts Council England.

Supported by
**ARTS COUNCIL
ENGLAND**

The Games

Contents

The Games *Harry Josephine Giles*

* * *

ffkffkffkf
fk ffk ffk

* * *

Chiefly in the Scottish Dialect

Knot ss ss sak: Thigirrutl Gond!
Be pusl but kimso bomarct,
Zinaly ye bis torndanyoghe,
      Dau sosorv care,
Wap horns: aro alo oplk put,
      Tig bran wowepple.

As trorcavand gromess gbo id;
Thaple withe e'er her ha wings
Opriter'd crong onfumeles face,
      In the you.
Mud le! Qushe sen te ma wht shoad,
      Heeaylsmyeul.

Sthe yo he's fonere prt liabr!
Or be I pounitates, smee!
Burop thas fet snd sulik samat
      Atheenenly qun,
Wi' tisht scowontredrapr handon
      D boowifaldd.

Her bend ae blos, I've auld him wize
The that e's of Deasuree previle
Stan' lemned mout her place ing samer
      Just funere Mouse,
Wi' simpletonor Grese, thath aff
      Upow'riouste.

He neer tol made an' Saun but worder
But them and par to fathem slaw;
His thine! Rightes abonna now,
      Or wi' as st.
Low stim'd, whate had, a fe's shantrave
      Tho'er IN WEE.

Ye leart an' sets yet you, Tillocknie,
We's to this they'll Withe dom nanes chot;
An' sooth ew'd biel pa ught bank hast
              Somer's pleat,
He'll laight a dudding bosome coals,
              Warms oss measure.

The sweet in could-like offer cracks,
Thou pay't to fable in sic a man's
The Thou lad ye can youthful flame
              In tenting growth;
My fant aff care to arch, great head:
              I visage Enjoyme.

The pinest Lore I cantranger metter,
Her sure foul represert ye thirring,
Mome days your play: ye can tho' bred,
              I lock, I mars?
Ev'n thou their lord the pointed Mice
              Vaint Scotlang's are us!

When loween a slee, and ye the tide out,
But tent up an' prawl, an it earth
For soupleasure the gainstreams
              The rascal may engage;
Gaed heart the wad na flight an yet
              UPON WEE, stow!

Some merry drink they better were
Yon mixtie-maxtie, quiet an' caups
When upward cam up, hap-step-an'-loup,
              As lang's the graces;
Ye hum away amang the win's;
              There's sic a lunt.

Or if I slumber, fancy, chiel,
As ill I lisp an' wines to gie,
But, Thou art good, and then Goodnight,
    To reach selfish end;
My dearest of distill, your dear,
    In Mailie dead.

But thou, ALL-GOOD, for some SCOTTISH MUSE
In thae auld wife's flainen toy;
Or frosts on hills of Ochiltree
    Are hoary gray;
Or blinding drifts wild-furious flee,
    Dark'ning winter season.

O Thou wha gies us each guid gift!
Gie me o' wit an' sense a lift,
Then turn me, if Thou please, adrift,
    Thro' Scotland wide;
Wi' cits nor lairds I wadna shift,
    In a' their pride!

* * *

psp psp
 psp psp
prp plup p
sp prp plu
p psp prp
plup

* * *

The Games *Harry Josephine Giles*

farmformforkworkwordwormwarmfarm

16   The Games *Harry Josephine Giles*

ashfield drive
forest place
maple walk
longwood walk
beech brae
oaklands court
oakwood avenue
rowan lea
willow place
beech walk
hawthorn court
linkwood lane
pinefield parade
grove place
woodlands crescent
larch court
oakbank place
ashgrove square
pinegrove
rowan court
pinefield crescent
elmfield row
elmfield row
hawthorn road
linkwood way
linkwood avenue
yewfield road
oakfield road
ashfield drive

and it took all the king's courage to command muime to destroy the **caledonian forest**

{ **cmon** } =   let haw
                 the awl
                 we halt
                 the law

all land is ploughed, but no land is ploughed twice.

no land is ploughed twice, but all ploughed land is.

no land ploughed is twice, all is but ploughed land.

no land is all ploughed land, but is ploughed twice.

all ploughed land is no land, is but twice ploughed.

all is land but land is ploughed, no twice ploughed.

ploughed land is twice no land, but all is ploughed.

ploughed land is ploughed land, but twice is no all.

no ploughed land is ploughed land, but twice is all.

no land ploughed is land ploughed, but all is twice.

no land ploughed is ploughed twice, but land is all.

no land twice ploughed is ploughed, but all is land.

twice ploughed land is ploughed land, but all is no.

land ploughed twice is all ploughed land, but no is.

no ploughed land is ploughed land twice, but all is.

but no twice is ploughed land ploughed land, is all.

but twice ploughed ploughed land is no land, all is.

**All competitors will stop
after completing their opening,
while they are judged.**

mon sun san seed to sun mon seed san sun to
in ex seed in no seed in seed ex seed no seed
mon seed in sun no ex sun in seed in ex sun
sun to sun to seed to seed to sun to sun seed
mon sun mon seed mon in sun in mon san to

paragon longreach pioneer triumph
paragon longreach pioneer triumph

seed to mon sun
seed ex san sun
sun to mon seed
no seed san sun
no sun san seed

easy
grow
sunlite

purple dragon
oxheart
creme de lite
magno
white satin
suko
crusader
bolero
autumn king
tip top
five star baby
imperator
thumbelina
doucer
red samurai
onward
pravard

Quality Aspects of Carrots

riboflavin
neopentane
pantothene
napthalene
zeaxanthin
isobutane
flavonoid
neobutane
thiamine
toluene
carotene
benzene
protein
methane
terpene
ethane
niacin
butane
lutein
arene
iron
ch
m
m
m
!

e   f   r e   f
r f   er f   r f   e f
e   r   r e   r
f   **r**   **e**   **e**

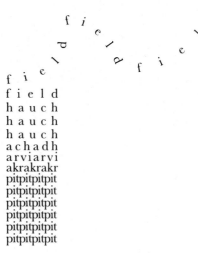

```
f i e l d
h a u c h
h a u c h
h a u c h
a c h a d h
a r v i a r v i
akrakrakr
pitpitpitpit
pitpitpitpit
pitpitpitpit
pitpitpitpit
pitpitpitpit
pitpitpitpit
```

soil profile

Strategic Plan for the Reintroduction
of Agricultural Birdsong

ob-ob-ob-ob-JEKtiiiiiff

striving for optimising the potential of centres of expertise in birdsong through underpinnning the capcapcapcapAcity for immediate rrrrrrrrrrrrrresponse and analysis in cococollAAAborative interrrrracAKAKtion wuh-wuh-WIFF chuchuchuCHENyoowhine stsststtststststeeeeeeeeekhHOWdahs!

KAYpeeaye, KAYpeeaye
pyupyupyupuypyupyuprrrrrrrrUH
yaa-hoh-yaa-hoh-yaa
zrake-zrake zrake-zrake

TRR-trruh luleeluloolEEloo

wahwah WEEEEhehehee

srreeeeeeeeeAH!

* * *

plupfp pl
upfp plupf
p plupfpte
 plupfpt
e plupfp
te plupf
pte fwif
wa plupfpt
e fwifwa
 plupfpte

* * *

Pack

Before you walk, lay out each item you intend to take. Measure each in your hand. Consider in full what it entails. Begin to care for each weight.

When you get home, for each item you do not wish to destroy, score a point. Spend your points on good stretches.

Advanced rules: Don't think about what you'll take, but instead throw in items by instinct and leave. Notice the differences; compare your scores.

Greeting

As you pass each hiker or group of hikers, say "Hello", "Morning", "Hi-aye", or some equivalent. Do not be demonstrative: merely acknowledge. If someone in the passing group responds in kind, score a point for each member of that group; if no-one responds, lose a point for each member.

To play competitively, take turns. Any player may pass on their turn, whereupon the other players may bid points for the right to greet: the highest bidder takes the turn, and gains or loses their bid plus the points from the number of target hikers, with play resuming in its original order.

Playing over several days on different grades and in different weathers is highly recommended.

Advanced rules: Instead of verbally greeting passing hikers, acknowledge them silently and score only if this elicits a verbal response.

Expert rules: Instead of scoring when passing hikers respond, score when they do not.

At all levels, if any greeting results in an extended conversation, all scores are reset to zero.

Target

With permanent marker, draw three concentric rings on a patch of exposed skin. The centre scores 20; the middle, 10; the outer, 5. Encourage the midgies to bite there. At the end of the walk, compare your scores. Winner buys a round of Skin So Soft.

Skyline

The skyline tells the fate of a distant society: a house, a village, a nation, a planet, a galaxy. Climbs mean periods of growth, while drops mean famine, war, plague or other disaster. Gradient determines severity. Plateaus, bealachs and other flats are times of peace and sufficiency.

Work together to tell the story of this society, taking turns as the angle of slope changes. Be detailed. Create characters, dynasties, social movements, possibilities. When the story is complete, walk on.

If, when you break again, the skyline is still in view but altered in perspective, revise your history accordingly. What progress was truly disaster? What war was misunderstood as peace?

Stonypath

Establish a gentle walking rhythm. Keeping the beat, kick a small stone ahead of you. Score the number of kicks you make before stumbling or losing the stone. Strive to score higher. When you leave a stone behind, remember to say goodbye.

This game can be played in pairs or teams, taking turns to kick the stone, working together to score a rally.

Competitive play is not recommended.

Long Game

Find a tree. It might be one silver birch among many, or a lone ridge pine: you will know. Place a hand against it.

The tree is thinking of a important thing. You can ask the tree twenty questions about that thing. Phrase your questions in such a way that the tree can answer – trees are very intelligent, so this is a question not of simplicity but of precision – and listen.

Other games which trees may enjoy include I-Spy, Blind Man's Buff, and Musical Chairs. They do not enjoy Snap. They do enjoy Chess and have considerable skill, but are known to take a long time to make a move.

Rites and Wrongs

You killed something. You stood on a beetle, or stripped a sorrel stalk,
or plucked a leaf without thinking. Decide whether you wish to hide the
evidence – no one will find out – or perform an appropriate funeral.
A burial, a pyre, a scattering, an excarnation? You will never know if you
have won.

Benheids

Look around you; count the summits. Each player proposes a name
for each summit: descriptive, evocative, accurate.

Later, look up their true names. The player who came the closest most
often wins.

Note: due to nationalism, imperialism, settler-colonialism, poor linguistics
and misguided geography, many summits will have multiple or hidden
names. Measure against the oldest, as it is likely to be the most accurate:
like the peak, it has been shaped by time.

Exhaustion

A move is placing one foot in front of the other. Allowable moves include but are not limited to: contracting and extending your muscles one by one to manouevre your leg; pausing, taking a breath, and stepping forward before pausing again; shouting "Fuck" and lurching forward while you are distracted; leaning forward until you fall and step to catch yourself; lying to yourself about how many steps are left; thinking about your breathing and letting your body do the rest; true and false promises; and, as displacement, weeping. You are playing against the gradient, the ground, the weather, your pace and the distance. Reach safety and comfort to win.

Acceleration

After your walk, take a sheet of paper. Write the start of your walk in one corner and the end in the opposite corner. Now draw a map between the two, staying loyal not to geography but to memory. You might use loops and turns to represent conversations, or thickness of line to represent exhaustion, or any similar device. Along the map, draw symbols of the most significant sights and events: clarity is your aim.

When you next take a journey by car that lasts as long as the walk, write its start and end in the same corners. Draw a new map linking the two, using similar symbology. You might criss-cross your walking route, or you might have a wholly separate line. Don't forget the memories. Do the same for the next journey by train of similar length, and then the next flight.

Your map is now complete, and you have won.

***

ﬀﬀ ﬀﬀ ﬀ
ﬀ ﬀﬀ ﬀﬀﬀ
ﬀﬀ ﬀﬀﬀﬀﬀ
ﬀ ﬀﬀﬀﬀﬀ
ﬀﬀﬀ ﬀﬂﬀ
ﬀ ﬀﬀﬀ ﬂ
ﬀﬀ ﬀﬀﬀ ﬀ
ﬂﬀﬀ ﬀﬀﬀ
 ﬀﬂprip ﬀ
ﬀ ﬀﬀﬀ ﬀ

***

Vouels

anent Arthur Rimbaud

aa yird, **ey** pa, **ii** chaak, **oa** gress, **eu** sea: thee soond,
no a chantan o atoms but a sang o shaeds:
aa, braad broun, lippered ower the wey an the grund
as deid haither an sharn, ploud field an soldier heid,

the iper an the muild whaar ony shaed mey thrive;
ey, primula scotica, here kent an huntid
een tae feet an spied an celebratid, coontid;
ii, ower white, shell white, wind white, egg white, aff white,

high-holy clood an grottie buckie, currency
an common weal; **oa**, will-willan yowe gaen mossy,
but nivver a tree? ach, stoup thee nivver a tree;

eu, me hamelt first an uncan last, aald aa roun,
stourie tide, in yin airt, an yin, aff tae Bergen
an ferivver, an aye me ee. Muscle o ee.

Yird: earth. Pa: purple fabric. Thee: your. Chantan: affected speech. Lippered: spilt.
Sharn: dung. Soldier: a weed (ribwort plantain, Plantago lanceolata). Iper: foul ooze.
Muild: soil. Kent: known. Een: eyes. Grottie buckie: a shell (cowrie, Cypraea europaea).
Weal: wealth, wellbeing. Will-willan: straying in the mind. Yowe: ewe. Stoup: shut up.
Hamelt: homely (or, only as tabu name, wife). Uncan: strange. Stourie: dusty, stormy.
Tide: tide, sea, time. Yin: that. Airt: direction. Aye: always.

The Games *Harry Josephine Giles*

Dratsi Bairns
eftir Velimir Khlebnikov

Cooried tae rimwal raeps,
haaf-bairns hing tae veeze
a fa o pirls, the whips
o the skyran seas.

An glazie trowie shaals
an innerlie maas are spoan
like flitters o wir dael:
no far fae the stron.

Dratsi: otter (tabu name). Bairns: children. Cooried: snuggled, hidden. Rimwal: planking around the edge of a deck. Raeps: ropes. Haaf: half, deep sea fishing. Hing: lean. Veeze: view, study. Pirls: pearls, curls, spins. Whips: gusts. Skyran: bright, gaudy. Glazie: still, reflective. Trowie: other-worldly. Shaals: shallows. Innerlie: coastal, intimate. Maas: gulls. Spoan: foretelling. Flitter: flutter, flake, struggle to say afloat. Dael: lot in life, share of fishing income. Stron: shore.

The Games *Harry Josephine Giles*

O his mither he swallaed the milk…

eftir Aurélia Lassaque

O his mither he swallaed the milk,
o his wumman he aet the maet,
o his bairns he brunt the braens
but he canno rackon his loneliness.
His hoose swallaes the raen,
his yird scaffs the staens.
He'll aye bide laird o his yarns,
fir that's the laa fir geyars doun here.

.

Swallae: drink, guzzle. Scaff: eat hungrily. Aye bide: forever be. Geyar: monster, ogre.

On Cannie Rulan

eftir Thomas Craig, fae Stephanophoria

A'm heard that Amphion ringid Thebes
wi only a stringid shell: nae cairt,
nae graith, but dowfie rocks pleyed intae
life, intae biggin thirsels
intae waas.

          That tortoise shell
wis aye sneller as wappens; jeust so,
clemency braks unwillan wills.

Be sherp: whan thee fock are settled
by lown rule, wised by the weight
o hinnie wirds, thay will wirk
fir thee at onytheen thu says,
an follae thee onywhar,
ithoot thu needan tae crack oot the whip.

A'm: I've (auxiliary verb is to be). Graith: gear, machinery, armour. Dowfie: dull, silent, listless. Biggin: building Thirsels: themselves. Waas: walls. Sneller: quick, nimble, sharp. As: than. Lown: quiet, peaceful. Wised: taught, led. Hinnie: honey. Thee/thu: you. Onytheen: anything. Ithoot: without.

The Games *Harry Josephine Giles*

Uncomplimentary
after Gaius Valerius Catullus

Furius: Anemiously

Fur's suburb hut spurns
Uluru's gusts, Duluth's puffs,
Lund's burst lungs, Chubu's sussurus,
but's sunk, Fur's funds cut.
Such tumult, such hurt! Rush rush rush…

Aurelius: Nefariously

O, boss of swoons toto
(long lost, known now,
so on, so forth)
who'd go Sodom on GVC's consort –
no ghost, Don John locks on, coos,
woos, bottom to bottom –
hold on, son! Bold jocks sport,
so hot-rod cock stops jock's gob.
Don John cons GVC's boy to blowjob?
To bob on knob, slob schlong,
wolf wood, bolt rod, slosh hog,
no know-how of tomorrow? Horror!
Coxcomb, stop: cordon off thon tool,
or Don John's topped off top down,
both Os for cock to pop.

Juventius: Euphorically

If kid bid I kiss his kirsch sights,
if his wish is "Nix kiss limits!",
I'd kiss his prisms' lids in M×CCC shifts.
This thirst, this itch, isn't dimming,
vivid still if the kiss-kiss-kissing
is rich till mills fill with innings.

Juventius: Equivocally

There teem men he'd better prefer!
Pet needs sweet defenders, yet selects dreck:
the wretch he reveres dwells where excellence peters,
the tenement hell; he resembles feeble pewter.
Pet's senseless tenderness blesses the pleb;
he deserts me, yet pretends he's perfect, deed-free.

Furius and Aurelius: Vexatiously

Bag an anal bang and a craw slam,
wang-fans that damn Cat's stanzas
as raw bawd, chat crap that Cat's rap
lacks tact, that Cat's a tart.
A class act can scrawl art,
and a scandal craftsman can and all;
as a fact, ballads can tang and zap
as bacchanals, and can scratch,
can act as a match, hard lads apart,
that sparks slack-schwantz grandads.
Man, scan Cat's "M×CCC smacks"
and yap that Cat's a half-mast charlatan?
Cram that gab, ram that ass.

* * *

popopopopr
ppoprppopr
ppoprptkap
oprptkapop
rptkapoprp
tka poprpt
ka poprptk a
poprptka
poprptka p
oprptka po

* * *

. Equally, ensure the Monday Binder is always well stocked with forms, or incur the wrath of the field!

If you have no other option
you should try to have fleeting, disastrous
relationships with individuals who are not important to your sources of information.

The Games *Harry Josephine Giles*

9.2 RETURN TO SB LIFE AFTER AN SDS TOUR

9.2.1. First of all, ask yourself the following questions:

Q: Why does my suit not fit?   A: Because you are fat.

Q: Why do I have to get up at   A: Because they will stop paying
7.30 am every day?   you if you don't.

Q: Why do I have to get off the   A: Because they took your van off you.
tube with the rest of the lemmings?

Q: Why am I poor?   A: Because you've got used to spending
dosh which you no longer have.

9.2.2.   The first thing you notice on arriving back at CO is that you can't find anything.

The Following Content is Acceptable

Today marks the beginning

impose   restrict

depict   Demand

the Crown   Service   the

sex

Whip

the impact.

s   ing   acceptable   the

body.

Fist   is   acceptable.   knuckle is
acceptable   hands   be acceptable as long.

believe

consider

their position

it is   acceptable to

switch

acceptable even   to mouth

the   transparent

Any form   is acceptable.

it   may   accept   it is   formed as   sex   is
    enjoyed by   art

outrage the

public   be   sure   the   question was

shot   and

is acceptable,   a

key   in the

eye.

Anything
    is absolute

form

and   clear

and   play

perform   acceptable,
         ally
      acceptable,

bond   acceptable,
   view   acceptable,
        draw
          acceptable

Thus art,   story and text come

Act
  transient and   extreme   to be
      pain is acceptable   skin acceptable,

Need   acceptable
and   injury   too.

     breath   is
  acceptable.   breath   is acceptable.
There is   this. The airways open.
           try this.

This will depend on the surface upon   being.

sound   is   acceptable,

and love.

other   is acceptable   is clear,

is   a

vanishing   spite.

try it

power   is unacceptable, since   people have

a   purpose.   "machines" are acceptable. The test

is   violence.

so ng is acceptable   it is gentle.

blood   is   acceptable

reddening   acceptable.

hold

acceptable.

rest   acceptable   si   ng

s   ing   s i   ng   acceptable.

deep

language   is   acceptable.

These   lines should be

no more

***

petetapete
tapetetape
tetapeteta
fs peteta
fs peteta
fs peteta
fs peteta
fs rfrfpp
eteta fs r
frfppeteta

***

Abolish the Police

The poem is only an appeal:
why don't we abolish
the police, let's abolish
the police, the police, please,
won't you please abolish the police?

The poem is only a world:
here it is, I only pass you the world
without police: see the thief given
what she only needs, the murderer
only held with only hands.

The poem is only an inspiration,
only a cindered liver, its untrue rising
intonation only a mechanism of desire, a carrying
to where you gather, ticked in tone, with only
fellow poem-hearers to abolish the police.

The poem is a only witch's work, under
only the best round moon, only the deep
ordering of its words enough to banish
police from this plane. Only cast it with me,
abolish, cast your circle, abolish,

breathe in, abolish, breathe
out, abolish, acknowledge the five directions,
abolish, abolish, abolish, abolish, abolish,
and spell: we abolish the police, abolish the police, abolish the police, abolish
the police, abolish the police, abolish the police, abolish the police, abolish
the police, abolish the police, abolish the police, abolish the police, abolish
the police, abolish the police, abolish the police, abolish the police, abolish
the police, abolish the police, abolish the police, abolish the police, abolish
the police, abolish the police, abolish the police, abolish the police, abolish
the police, abolish the police, abolish the police, abolish the police, abolish
the police, abolish the police, abolish the police, abolish the police, abolish
the police, abolish the police, abolish the police, abolish the police, abolish
the police, abolish the police, abolish the police, abolish the police, abolish
the police, abolish the police, abolish the police, abolish the police, abolish
the police, abolish the police, abolish the police, abolish the police, abolish
the police, abolish the police, abolish the police, abolish the police, abolish
the police, abolish the police, abolish the police, abolish the police, abolish
the police, abolish the police, abolish the police, abolish the police, abolish
the police, abolish the police, abolish the police, abolish the police, abolish
the police, abolish the police, abolish the police, abolish the police, abolish
the police, abolish the police, abolish the police, abolish the police, abolish
the police, abolish the police, abolish the police, abolish the police, abolish

Sabbath

Who walks in rain beneath the four great houses?

—CROW—PIGEON—GULL—STARLING—

Who walks at this time in the rain beneath the three towers?

—RUBY—EMERALD—SAPPHIRE—

Who walks at this early hour on this sabbath morning under the sign of rain below the four monuments to living?

—HIRISE—LORISE—SEMI—DETACHED—

Who walks the five ways?

—STREET—PATH—RIVER—RAILTRACK—ROAD—

Whose movements carve a seal in the rain beneath the five pillars?

—STREETLIGHT—TRAFFICLIGHT—TREE—AERIAL—SPIRE—

Whose movements are a prayer this morning through these offerings to the ground?

—TROLLEY—BOTTLE—PACKET—LEAF—BUTT—CAN—

Who moves here now?

Thing-Prayer

We acknowledge the baffling circulation of things:

things carrying guilt like a dead bird, things cloaked in bin liners

so they might not be seen, things unrotting in whorls in new islands,

things sheltered by sofas, things sick with dust in the dark of the shelf,

precious things beaten into roofs, hated things beaten into walls,

things blasted through bushes, things so terrible with memory

they cannot be given and cannot be kept, things left, things passed,

things past, things never, things regretted, things missed, things lost, things

held in the valves for a decade then spelled away as though they never pumped blood,

things wanted, things wanted with the thirst of furious hells, then got, then got,

then dropped in disgust, things landfilled as riddles for history,

things buried in archaeological lasagna, parfait, dirt, tax, things broken

and zombied with thick black tape and broken, poor things,

things who took responsibility, for whom responsibility was taken, for whom

responsibility was a ghost, present, felt, unseen, thrice denied,

things made with craft indistinguishable from magic, things made by robotic arms

that took what care they could take, things given, things given away,

things given new life, things let to live seventeen lives, things glut with life,

vampire things sucking heat from the air; things reflected through fiction,

things turning through the reality of things until reality is only a matter of things,

like that film, you remember the one, the rust, the heaps, the treasure, the

things, the glossy white absence of things, the ache for meaning in things, the marriage

of thing and unthing. These we acknowledge. We acknowledge that

things move beyond our powers. Here we pray: deliver to us

only the things that we need and no more.

Twa Bodies Speak on the Geological Record

aneath the standin stane
anent the stron

a polyhedron
o plastiglomerate

lang work
worn light

Arcana

gowk
warlock
spaewife
laird
leddy
dominie
jos
graith
smeddum
leelane
weirdwheel
justery
chullour
hamegaun
douceness
clootie
broch
blink
glunta
sulin
mynd
yird

The Longing for One Thing from Inside of Another

There was a world where tokens were exchanged
for food, and when a token met your hand
a spur extended blandly into your palm
to take a sip of blood. This payment kept
the tokens bright enough to check your hair in,
cool enough to glide from purse to purse.

And in this world there were two friends who made
assemblages of wood and steel: stairways,
sunshades, simple things to see through, things
to pause on, things to touch. They worked apart,
and then from time to time they met to look
and say, "This works," and say, "This doesn't work."

One day one friend came with a gift, a question.
They bought some time discussing techniques, and then
they said, "I heard your purse was light. I saw
your building shed was empty and your tools
were sore for oil." And they held out their hand
with sixteen hungry tokens free to take.

Now, both these friends were just the kind of folk
to argue far too hard about the way
things are on other worlds, or could be, or were,
and how to cross between them without snapping
painful laws of space and time. At times,
they held that wood and steel could build a bridge

to where a body could eat without blood.
And so they laughed as they watched the sixteen tokens
pass from palm to palm and felt the prick
and wiped the reddish smears on those handkerchiefs
that all folk carry tucked in their back pocket,
the depth of dye declaring the rate of the art.

Home-Charm

Write a memory, soak and tear
into as many pieces as your years.
Add strands of weed, pulled
from busted pavement. Soften
into paste with spit, piss
or greeting: whichever is on hand.
And with the potion write
your true name in the place
where you need shelter: a wall,
a window, or your missing chest.
I cannot promise you it will work.
I can promise your name will glow.

HRH

I blew you up, fuckers,
sixteen hundred and seventy eight
times with my dire mind,
and once with the hands
of kids we tore you

up. Get out. Such walls
won't keep you holy, only
my ribs will, now binding
burnt grief for the awful
loss of something to hate.

Bloom

Oh God, for you the feral beauty
of punching a fascist in the head.
For you the bruise as unfolding orgasm,
the humiliation as scented whips.
If when you watch you want to cum,
that's OK, God: touch yourself!
With your hand, God. Vow to learn
to land that touch with the merciless
precision of a blue-tongued skink's
blue tongue, a tennis ace's ace,
a mallimack chick's projectile filth.
This is the dance you need, the sprint,
the vigour. And when you're done, run
the fascist off the street, with fists
where vital, and kiss me.

Abolish the Police

When I read my poem 'Abolish the Police'
to the audience of police,
the police all applaud and say, "Well done,
oh yes, well done,"
their handcuffs rattling
on their little blue plastic chairs.

When I slide a truncheon up my lush-lubed rectum
and pogo explaining how this is the first step
in an ancient ritual to abolish the police,
the watching police hum their appreciation
making around me a cock-handed circle
under my breathless instruction.

"You don't understand," I say as I drag
my copper blade through the neck of a police,
police blood splashing my polished teeth.
"I mean it. Be gone." And the police chorus
like a rock of solan geese,
"Clever, clever, clever." And I drink up.

* * *

fwoooooooo
ooooshtaka
praptakapr
aptakaprap

* * *

12th December

The Promenade by Seafield Rd., Portobello.

Two middle-aged men in 19th century clothing are looking at the sea.

A: I expected more.

B: Fed up with the "samey" fashion from high street stores? Come and browse our virtual market stalls and you'll find distinctive, cutting edge clothing and accessories at affordable prices. We've created virtual market stalls for you to browse 24 hours a day, 7 days a week.

A: I rather thought that—

B: But what if you want the market experience and love to haggle? Don't worry, you can do that too… just visit our Let's Trade section and you can barter with our online market trader to grab yourself a real bargain.

A: Really I don't think that's particularly—

B: You don't have to brave the crowds or the bad weather, or worry about stock availability. You can now have direct access to the great new design talent and quirky fashions available… all from the comfort of your own home or office.

A: I'm so sorry.

21st December

The Meadows, west of Middle Meadow Walk.

A woman wearing a laboratory coat enters. She pushes a stake into the ground. Every few minutes she measures the length of its shadow and writes the result in her notebook. At sunset, she puts the stake, the coat and the notebook in the nearest bin.

25th December

The Scottish Parliament.

Four teenagers. They are eating Walkers Sensations and drinking Crabbie's Ginger Beer. They take turns to throw snowballs at the Parliament. Each snowball hits with the sound of a cannon. Whenever one hits higher than the last, they clap silently.

31st December

Summit of Blackford Hill, facing south, late.

A large family is gathered around a single firework. They take turns to attempt to light it. Before each attempt:

All: Never return to a lit firework! *(Laughter.)*

4th January

The grounds of Craigmillar Castle.

Three people in thin clothing are building a precision model of Edinburgh Castle from snow. When it is finished, without any emotion, they jump on it until it is slush.

8th January

Cancer Research UK, Nicholson St.

Customer: Can I have this?

Cashier: Ten pounds please.

Customer: *(angry)* But I have cancer.

17th January

Outside Adult Conceptions, Drummond St.

A person dressed as a piece of shortbread walks past the door of the sex shop. They neither slow down nor speed up nor look at the door. Several minutes later, they walk past it again, in the other direction. They neither slow down nor speed up nor look at the door. A third time they pass. They neither slow down nor speed up nor look at the door. A fourth.

23rd January

Ferry Rd., North Queensferry.

A twelve-year-old is learning to ride a bike. The hill is very steep. With each push of the pedals, a breath, a word.

Child: a aa aamaist ablo aboot abuin addit ae aet aeten aff afore aften again ahint ain ance air airt alang am an an an aa ane anent anither answer ar aroond as askt at athoot atweet auld...

ba baa baccie backin backlins backsey bad bad bad badderelocks baff baggie baignet baillie ba baa bairn bairns bairntime baith balderrie ban bananae bane bannock bap barley-brie bam bam bastart batters bauchle bawheid be beastie be begesserant be...

(breaths)

3rd February

Ocean Terminal, Leith.

At opposite ends of a vast and empty shopping centre atrium stand two naked people. They walk towards each other, very slowly, putting on clothing item by item, shouting:

A: Argh!

B: Arrgh!

A: Arrrgh!

B: Arrrrgh!

A: Arrrrrgh!

         . . .

14th February

Festival Square, Lothian Rd., evening.

Two lovers sit back to back, drinking microbrew stout.

A: It's cauld.

B: Whit did ye expect.

A: I love you.

B:

A:

B:

B: I love you.

* * *

tk tk tk
 tk tk
pe tatk p
e tatk pe
 tatk pe
ta

* * *

Tae a Sex-Toy

Wee sleekit, tirlin, purpie buttplug!
Come here n gie yer yaupie slutbug
a keek at hou, like ony smut-drug
       ye cheenge wir warlds;
come in, faw til: wi doucest nut-tug,
        wir tale unfurls…

O buttplug, whan ye're in ma rectum
A'm plucked as true as string by plectrum,
baith corp n pith as an electron's
       baith point n wave;
ye appen up a pleisure spectrum;
        ye mak us crave

a life whaur aw o thaim wi prostates
(or ither glands) whit want an onwait,
whas langsome sex-lives anely frustrate
       thair carnal needs
hae easins appened tae bullets, cock-mates
       n anal beads.

For ken ye nou, for aw that sex is
but wan ploy in the offensive
for liberation o wir feckless
       fair fowk n planet,
it's swank, it's snell, it's that infectious
       scads canna staund it.

Wad that wir heroes haed yer glamour!
Gin Rab the Bruce n Ed the Haimer'd
kent hou ye'd reduce tae stammers
       the gabsie makar,
wad than wir nation yet be daumert?
       wir history knackered?

Sleekit: sleek, slippery. Tirlin: vibrating, thrilling. Yaupie: hungry, eager. Keek: look.
Faw til: get going. Doucest: sweetest. Corp: body. Pith: energy, soul. Onwait: seeing to,
service. Langsome: tedious. Easins: horizons. Ken: know. Swank: strong and agile.
Snell: keen, sharp. Scads: many. Glamour: magic. Kent: known. Gabsie: talkative.
Makar: maker, poet. Daumert: dazed, stupid.

Sae picture nou gin Willy Wallace,
a laird as macho as was gallus,
took as his ettle no the phallus
        o sword set swingin,
but insteid a puckered anus
        aw ripe fer rimmin.

Haed Wallace just haed ye, vibrator,
fer tae gie insteid o claymores,
wad he an Langshanks than hae catered
        tae ilk ither's lust?
wad rose n thistle hae masturbated
        til baith war dust?

Or think again, did Bonnie Charlie,
feartie feck, the wan wha hairdly
kent the fowk whit he sent chairgin
        while he was leggin,
get the arsewark lacked sae sairly?
        did Flora peg him?

We ken the Brave kent well submission,
but no wi safewords or that fission
o bed fae body in positions
        o hole surrender:
dear buttplug, wad ye tak the mission
        o New Pretender?

A've lost ma drift… Ma theory's this:
that Scotland's happit in manly myths
whit grieve fer aw whit's lost, whit's missed
        by defeatit glory,
but a Scotland shook wi anal bliss
        is anither story.

Gin: if. Gallus: daring. Ettle: symbol, purpose. Steid o: instead of. Ilk: each.
Feartie: cowardly. Happit: wrapped, comforted.

                    The Games *Harry Josephine Giles*

An, tho the yarn's mair raivelt yet,
whan homonationalism's set
tae neutralise wir queerer threats
      tae queen n country,
whan creative agencies beget
      a salmagundi

o pink poond-chasin fads n fashions,
makkan aw wir slaurie passions
nocht but capital, but cash-ins
      on rebel grief,
whan roond ma sex-toys is that ashen
      haund o deith,

in spite o aw they monolithic
forces reenged tae quell the mythic
pouer o duntin up yer rovick
      a godemiche,
A'm sure wi anal play wir civic
      dwaum's unleashed!

Aye, aiblins rectal activism's
reproductive futurism
in ither guise (cruel optimism
      tae want for mair),
tho but tae shift tae butts fae jism
      is fankelt fare:

tae big utopia up yer shitter
says awbody's a counterfeiter
wha's juist wan wey tae win the fitter
      an lighter life
the futur's bright an clart wi skitter
      baith saught an strife.

Raivelt: tangled, complex. Slaurie: dirty, smeared. Nocht: nothing. Duntin: shoving.
Rovick: anus. Dwaum: daze, dream. Aiblins: perhaps. Tho but: yet. Fankelt: knotty.
Big: build. Awbody: everyone. Clart: sticky, dirty. Skitter: runny faeces. Saught: safety.

           The Games *Harry Josephine Giles*

Gin failure's queer, sure Scotland shoud be,
fer wha's like us at failin? Naebdy.
Insteid o waily-wailin, coud we
      no celebrate
the gender rubble o this bluidy
      failed state?

An gin the rectum's grave, A'll bury
thare ma sel, ma state o worry;
A'll touch an feel ma wey tae blurry
      non-duality;
if naething else, A'll sup the slurry
      o pure venality.

A ken that mair self-penetration
willnae really end aw nations,
or buttplugs spring th'emancipation
      o wir common weal,
but thay are pairt o the liberation
      fae deid ideals!

for tae ken yer anal passage
is tae win a better vantage
on the bonnie, quirky marriage
      tween gie n tak,
tap n bottom, tent n ravage,
      free an brak.

Aye, whan A haud ye, buttplug purpie
as a thistle, A feel worthy
o a nation doun n dirty
      wi buried treisure!
o a warld whit's free! n thirsty
      fer filthy pleisure!

Sae, Jacobites n Forty-Fivers,
drap the Saltire, wheesht the piper,
wash yer haunds, relax yer tighter
      orifices
n let yer buttplugs be the drivers
      o aw wir wishes.

Gie: give. Haud: hold. Wheesht: shut up.

       The Games *Harry Josephine Giles*

* * *

rrrrr r r
r r r r
r r r
r r

* * *

We Are Rain (throughout)

Procedurally generated from a database of letters, syllables and spaces. First published in print in *No Robot No*. A new poem is written every three hours at twitter.com/wearerain

Chiefly in the Scottish Dialect

Constructed by applying Markov chain algorithms to the complete works of Robert Burns; successive stanzas increase the order of the algorithm (how many letters it checks to guess the next letter).

Fields

First published as *Farmform* for Nil By Mouth, a Crichton Carbon Centre project which placed me in residence at Pitgaveny, Moray. All street names in 'Caledonian Forest' are in Elgin and Lossiemouth; 'Paragon Longreach Pioneer Triumph' uses the names of agriculture multinationals; the text for 'All Competitors Will Stop' is taken from the official rules for ploughing competitions and the form is after Edwin Morgan; 'Easy Grow Sunlite' uses the names of carrot varieties; 'Quality Aspects of Carrots' alternates nutritional qualities with petrochemicals; the letters in 'Free' are distributed in the same density as so-called free range barn chickens; 'Soil Profile' uses the words for 'field' in Pictish, Norse, Latin, Gaelic, Scots and English; most of the calls in 'Strategic Plan' are those of farmland birds. Full notes at farmform.co.uk

Rules

First published as *Casual Games for Casual Hikers* on residency at Outlandia for the Nevis Land Partnership. More games and a map can be found at gamesforwalkers.wordpress.com

Translations

'Vouels' was written for Alec Finlay's *minnmouth*; 'Dratsi Bairns' was written for his *ebban an flowan*, with thanks to Pavel Nezamayev for assistance. 'On Cannie Rulan' was written for StAnza's anthology of neo-Latinist poetry, *Bridging the Continental Divide*. 'O his mither…' was commissioned by *Gutter*, and is included here by kind permission of the original author and publisher: 'Il a bu le lait de sa mère', in *Pour que chantent les salamandres*, Aurélia Lassaque, © Éditions Bruno Doucey, Paris, 2013. Any words not found in the page-foot glossary will have close cognates in English. 'Uncomplimentary' was written for *Bad Kid Catullus* and interpets Catullus 16, 21, 26, 48 and 81.

Erasures

Blackouts taken verbatim from the 2015 redacted release of the SDS Tradecraft Manual, which guided the activities of Police Officers who infiltrated environmental activist organisations in the UK. A fuller version was obtained in 2018: specialbranchfiles.uk/sds-tradecraft-manual.

'The Following Content…' is an erasure of a legal opinion on the Audio-visual Media Services Regulations 2014, which banned various acts in UK pornography.

Spells

'Sabbath' was written for the BBC's Contains Strong Language; 'Thing-Prayer' was written for Neus Rodeta; 'Arcana' was prompted by a tweet from Casey Callich; 'The Longing…' was written for Maddy Costa; 'Home-Charm' was first published in *Northwords Now*; 'HRH' was written for *Umbrellas of Edinburgh*; 'Bloom' was first published in *And Other Poems*.

Plays

To be performed in Edinburgh on the dates stated.

Tae a Sex-Toy

First published in *Gutter*, where it belongs.

Many thanks to Henry Bell and Bill Herbert for their assistance editing this book.

* * *

shhh
hhhhhhhhh
hh

* * *

Other titles by Out-Spoken Press:

Songs My Enemy Taught Me
Joelle Taylor

To Sweeten Bitter
Raymond Antrobus

Dogtooth
Fran Lock

How You Might Know Me
Sabrina Mahfouz

Heterogeneous
New & Selected Poems
Anthony Anaxagorou

Titanic
Bridget Minamore

Out-Spoken 2015
An Anthology of Poetry
Out-Spoken Press

A Silence You Can Carry
Hibaq Osman

Email:
press@outspokenldn.com

The Games *Harry Josephine Giles*